Pebble®

Dogs

Siberian Huskies

by Gillia M. Olson

Consulting Editor: Gail Saunders-Smith, PhD

Consultant: Jennifer Zablotny, DVM
Member, American Veterinary Medical Association

Capstone
press®

Mankato, Minnesota

Pebble Books are published by Capstone Press,
151 Good Counsel Drive, P.O. Box 669, Mankato, Minnesota 56002.
www.capstonepress.com

1 2 3 4 5 6 12 11 10 09 08 07

Library of Congress Cataloging-in-Publication Data
Olson, Gillia M.
    Siberian huskies / by Gillia M. Olson.
    p. cm.—(Pebble Books. Dogs)
    Summary: "Simple text and photographs present an introduction to the Siberian
husky breed, its growth from puppy to adult, and pet care information"—Provided
by publisher.
    Includes bibliographical references and index.
    ISBN-13: 978-1-4296-0017-0 (hardcover)
    ISBN-10: 1-4296-0017-9 (hardcover)
    1. Siberian husky—Juvenile literature. I. Title. II. Series.
SF429.S65O47 2008
636.73—dc22   2006100685

Note to Parents and Teachers

The Dogs set supports national science standards related to life
science. This book describes and illustrates Siberian huskies.
The images support early readers in understanding the text. The
repetition of words and phrases helps early readers learn new
words. This book also introduces early readers to subject-specific
vocabulary words, which are defined in the Glossary section. Early
readers may need assistance to read some words and to use the
Table of Contents, Glossary, Read More, Internet Sites, and Index
sections of the book.

Table of Contents

4

Sled Dogs

Siberian huskies
are sled dogs.
They pull sleds
long distances
in cold, snowy weather.

Huskies first came
from Siberia, a cold place
in northern Russia.
Thick fur
keeps them warm.

From Puppy to Adult

Even as puppies,
huskies have thick coats.

Many huskies have
markings that look
like a mask.
Their fur color ranges
from white to red
to black.

Many huskies have
bright blue eyes.
Some have brown eyes
or one blue and
one brown eye.

Adult huskies
are medium-sized dogs.
Their backs rise
to just past
a person's knees.

Husky Care

Huskies need food
made for active dogs.
They also need
plenty of fresh water.

Huskies shed all the time.
They shed the most
in spring and fall.
Owners should brush
huskies' coats daily.

Siberian husky owners enjoy active, independent dogs. With good care, huskies make loving pets.

Glossary

active—being able to exercise, play, and move around

coat—a dog's fur

distance—the amount of space between two places

independent—having the quality of not needing or wanting much help

markings—patches of color

shed—to lose fur; Siberian huskies shed all the time but more in spring and fall.

sled—a piece of wood or other material that is used to ride over snow and ice; Siberian huskies pull sleds.

Read More

London, Jonathan. *Sled Dogs Run.* New York: Walker, 2005.

Stone, Lynn M. *Siberian Huskies.* Eye to Eye with Dogs. Vero Beach, Fla.: Rourke, 2005.

Internet Sites

FactHound offers a safe, fun way to find Internet sites related to this book. All of the sites on FactHound have been researched by our staff.

Here's how:

1. Visit *www.facthound.com*

2. Choose your grade level.

3. Type in this book ID **1429600179** for age-appropriate sites. You may also browse subjects by clicking on letters, or by clicking on pictures and words.

4. Click on the **Fetch It** button.

FactHound will fetch the best sites for you!   23

Index

Word Count: 134
Grade: 1
Early-Intervention Level: 18

Editorial Credits
Becky Viaene, editor; Juliette Peters, set designer; Kim Brown, book designer;
Kara Birr, photo researcher; Karon Dubke, photographer; Kelly Garvin, photo stylist

Photo Credits
Capstone Press/Karon Dubke, 12, 14, 16, 18, 20; Cheryl A. Ertelt, 4; Lynn M. Stone, 8;
Mark Raycroft, cover; Shutterstock/Amanda Boutcher, 6; Shutterstock/Jeffrey Van Daele,
1; Shutterstock/pixshots, 10

Capstone Press thanks Bob and Dakota Bomier with Pet Expo in Mankato, Minnesota,
and dog trainer Martha Diedrich, for their assistance with this book.